EMILY POST'S
WEDDING PLANNER

REVISED EDITION

ELIZABETH L. POST

a keepsake of the wedding of

Colleen Scaglione

and

Craig Braun

on

_____

at

_____

Designer: C. Linda Dingler

ISBN 0-06-273018-5

Dear Bride and Groom,

That very special day that belongs to the two of you is fast approaching, and with it, the myriad of decisions and preparations which are a part of it. This planner is designed to help the two of you organize your thoughts and all the things that need to be done so that you can relax and enjoy this wonderful time. In the midst of all the excitement, remember that it is important for you to take time away from your preparations to spend with each other.

This planner is for the bride's mother, too, and those who are involved in your wedding plans. The records you keep here will be invaluable as she and they organize their responsibilities. Remember, though, that this is *your* wedding and the final decisions are yours. Both of you may want to consult your parents, both to include them and to take full advantage of their interest and experience, but this wedding belongs to the two of you.

I suggest that you glance through the planner before beginning to use it. It is arranged to have important names and telephone numbers at the very beginning so you can always find them easily, but do begin with the Bride's Check List on page 11 and the Budget Planner section which begins on page 43 so that you know precisely what you need to to first, and the resources you will have available to do them.

I wish you both great happiness on your wedding day, and throughout all the years ahead.

Sincerely,

Elizabeth L. Post

You will want to consult with members of your families and your bridal party during your wedding planning. Use these pages to list everyone: both sets of parents, and any stepparents involved in your wedding, brothers and sisters; all the members of your bridal party, and other friends or relatives you'll need to be in touch with. Even though you may have their addresses and telephone numbers in another address book, listing them here gives you instant access to the way to reach them. Be sure to list both home and business phone numbers since you might need to reach someone during the day.

Name	*Address*	*Telephone*

Name	Address	Telephone

Name	Address	Telephone

Name	Address	Telephone

Ready Reference for Professional Resources

Further along in this planner you'll find pages to help you decide which professionals will help make your wedding a truly memorable occasion and spaces for recording specific details of your arrangements with them. Once you have selected your reception site, caterer, florist, photographer, videographer and musician(s), record their names, addresses and telephone numbers below to keep this information always at your fingertips. Always obtain the name of the person who will be handling your wedding at each establishment so that you will know whom to contact when you call.

Reception site

       Name:
       Address:
       Telephone:

       Manager:

Caterer

       Name:
       Address:
       Telephone:

       Banquet manager:

Florist

    Name:
    Address:
    Telephone:

    Person to contact:

Photographer

    Name of studio:
    Address:
    Telephone:

    Photographer assigned to your wedding:

    Time photographer is to arrive at the wedding:

Musician

    Name of band:
    Agent's name:
    Address:
    Telephone:

    Person to contact:

Videographer

Name of studio:
Address:
Telephone:

Cameraperson assigned to your wedding:

Time cameraperson is to arrive at the wedding:

Bakery (if ordering cake separately)

Name:
Address:
Telephone:

Person to contact:

Stationery store or printer for invitations and announcements

Name: *Pony X Press*
Address: *Rt. 9 Bayville*
Telephone: *269-2345*
(Fax#) 269-1919
Person to contact: *Craig Velardi*

Bride's Check List

The best organized weddings are the ones where every detail has been thought of in advance. Thinking of those details is only the first step, however. Keeping a master check list, whether this one or one you write yourself, ensures that nothing is left to chance.

Your timetable should start three to six months before your wedding, and your master check list should be kept in a convenient place where you can consult it regularly, checking off items as they are attended to and adding even more details that may be special to your plans.

Three to six months in advance of your wedding:

- ☑ Decide on the type of wedding and reception you want
- ☐ Consult your priest or rabbi to select the date and hour of your wedding
- ☐ Determine the location of your reception and reserve the club, hotel, restaurant or hall if it is not to be at home
- ☐ Engage a caterer if your reception is to be at home
- ☐ Determine the number of guests you are able to invite
- ☑ Choose attendants and ask them to serve
- ☑ Order invitations and announcements
- ☐ If you wish, order notepaper for thank-you notes, some monogrammed with your current initials and some monogrammed with your married initials for later on

Three months in advance of your wedding:

- ☐ With your fiancé, make appointments for counseling with your priest or rabbi and for discussing music, decorations and procedures during the ceremony with the priest or rabbi, sexton and organist
- ☐ Order your gown and those of your attendants
- ☐ Make out your guest list and ask the groom and his family to send you theirs. Tell them approximately how many guests they may invite
- ☐ Make an appointment with a photographer for your formal portraits and reserve his or her time for the day and time of your ceremony and reception
- ☐ If you plan to have live music at your reception, hire the band or the musician, or a disk jockey if you plan to have taped music for dancing

- [ ] If your wedding will be at home, make arrangements now for repairs, painting, cleaning, etc.
- [ ] Begin shopping for your personal and household trousseaus
- [ ] Select china, crystal and silver patterns
- [ ] Select gifts for your bridesmaids and a gift for your groom if you intend to give him one

Two months in advance of your wedding:

- [ ] Hire limousines, if necessary, for transporting the bridal party to the ceremony and from the ceremony to the reception
- [ ] Notify your attendants about their fittings and accessories. If possible, have shoes dyed in one lot
- [ ] With your groom, if possible, list your selections at local gift and department store bridal registries. Tell your mother and your maid of honor where you are registered so that they can tell guests who ask them
- [ ] At the time of, or soon after, the final fitting of your wedding dress, have formal bridal photographs taken
- [ ] Make detailed arrangements with the manager of your reception site or caterer including menu, table arrangements, decorations, linens, parking, and so on
- [ ] Make medical and dental appointments, and a hairdresser appointment if you intend to have your hair done on the day of your wedding
- [ ] Address and stuff wedding invitations
- [ ] Make housing arrangements for out-of-town attendants and obtain hotel and motel information for guests from out of town
- [ ] With your groom, select wedding rings
- [ ] Mail invitations four to six weeks in advance of your wedding
- [ ] Remind your groom or the best man to arrange fittings and reserve any rented formalwear for himself and the groomsmen

One month in advance of your wedding:

- [ ] Check with your groom about his blood test and the marriage license
- [ ] If you are displaying wedding gifts, begin setting up tables for them
- [ ] Record all gifts and write thank-you's as they arrive

- [ ] Make a list of your honeymoon clothing and be sure it is cleaned, pressed and ready to pack
- [ ] Check on all accessories for you and your attendants
- [ ] Make final arrangements with all professionals who are working with you—florist, photographer, reception manager or caterer
- [ ] If you are changing your name, do so on all documents such as driver's license, credit cards and bank accounts
- [ ] Check your luggage to be sure it is adequate and in good condition
- [ ] Check on the advisability of a floater insurance policy to cover your wedding gifts—especially if you are displaying them
- [ ] Arrange the details for a bridesmaid's luncheon if you wish to give one
- [ ] Address your announcements, stamp them, and give them to your mother or a friend to mail the day after your wedding
- [ ] Make the arrangements for a place for your bridesmaids to dress
- [ ] Plan the seating for the bridal table and parents' table(s) at your reception and make out place cards for them
- [ ] Send your wedding announcement to the newspapers with your wedding portrait, if you wish
- [ ] Notify your wedding party of the time of the rehearsal

Two weeks in advance of your wedding:

- [ ] Confirm hotel, motel or other lodging arrangements for your bridal party
- [ ] Confirm flower order and deliveries with florist

One week in advance of your wedding:

- [ ] Pick up gifts for your attendants
- [ ] Give final count of guests to reception manager or caterer
- [ ] Reserve afternoon to have friends and family visit to view your gifts, if on display
- [ ] Plan quiet dinner for just you and your fiancé
- [ ] Plan light refreshments for your attendants if they will be changing at your house

The day of your wedding:

IN THE MORNING:

☐ Have hair done, or shampoo and arrange it yourself
☐ Make sure any orders not being delivered are picked up (flowers, food, etc.)
☐ Eat breakfast—no matter how nervous you may be

TWO HOURS BEFORE THE CEREMONY:

☐ Have your attendants arrive at your house to prepare to dress and to assist you with any last-minute details
☐ Meet your attendants at the hotel, if you will be changing there instead, or one hour before at a reserved room at the place your ceremony will be held

ONE HOUR BEFORE THE CEREMONY:

☐ Apply make-up and dress, making sure to cover face before dressing so as not to get make-up on your gown
☐ Ushers should arrive at the site at least 45 minutes before the ceremony, to plan duties and to seat early arrivals

ONE HALF HOUR BEFORE THE CEREMONY:

☐ Groom and best man arrive at place of ceremony
☐ Background music starts
☐ First guests arrive and are seated
☐ If you have dressed at home, you and your attendants go to church or synagogue and wait in private room
☐ Best man checks last-minute arrangements with priest or rabbi and gives him or her the fee

FIFTEEN MINUTES BEFORE THE CEREMONY:

☐ Family members and honored guests (godparents, for example) arrive and are seated "within the ribbon" or in the pews near the front

FIVE MINUTES BEFORE THE CEREMONY:

☐ The groom's mother and father arrive and she is escorted to her seat, followed by her husband

- [ ] The bride's mother is escorted to her seat in the front row
- [ ] The white carpet, or aisle runner, is rolled down the aisle
- [ ] The bride's father takes his place with his daughter
- [ ] The attendants take their places in the proper order for the processional
- [ ] At precisely the time stated on the invitation, the music starts and the ushers lead the procession down the aisle

First Big Decisions

Before you begin planning the smaller details, there are certain major decisions which must be made as soon as you start to plan your wedding. You must decide whether you wish to have a small or a large wedding, a formal or an informal wedding, and where you want it to take place. You will also want to invite your attendants immediately. These three pages present various options and allow you space to make notes. Greater detail on clothing for you, your attendants, family members and guests is listed on pages 34 and 35.

	Formal	*Semiformal*	*Informal*
Bride's dress	Long white gown, train, veil optional	Long white gown, veil optional	White or pastel cocktail dress or suit or afternoon dress (sometimes, very simple long gown)
Bridesmaids' dresses	Long or according to current style	Long or according to current style	Same type of dress as worn by bride
Dress of groom and his attendants	Cutaway or tailcoat	Sack coat or tuxedo	Dark blazer or jacket
Bride's attendants	Maid or matron of honor, 4–10 bridesmaids, flower girl, ring bearer (optional)	Maid or matron of honor, 2–6 bridesmaids, flower girl, ring bearer (optional)	Maid or matron of honor, 1 or 2 bridesmaids (optional)
Groom's attendants	Best man; 1 usher for every 50 guests, or same number as bridesmaids	Best man; 1 usher for every 50 guests, or same number as bridesmaids	Best man; 1 usher if necessary to seat guests

	Formal	*Semiformal*	*Informal*
Location of ceremony	Church, synagogue, or large home or garden	Church, synagogue, chapel, hotel, club, home, garden	Chapel, rectory, justice of the peace, home, garden
Location of reception	Club, hotel, garden, or large home	Club, restaurant, hotel, garden, home	Church parlor, home, restaurant
Number of guests	200 or more	75 to 200	75 or under
Provider of service at reception	Caterer at home, or club or hotel facilities	Caterer at home, or club or hotel facilities	Caterer, friends and relatives, or restaurant
Food	Sit-down or semi-buffet (tables provided for bridal party, parents, and guests); hot meal served; wedding cake	Buffet (bridal party and parents may have tables); cocktail buffet food, sandwiches, cold cuts, snacks, wedding cake	Stand-up buffet or 1 table for all guests; may be a meal or snacks and wedding cake
Beverages	Champagne; whiskey and soft drinks (optional)	Champagne or punch for toasts; whiskey and soft drinks (optional)	Champagne or punch for toasts; tea, coffee, or soft drinks in addition

	Formal	*Semiformal*	*Informal*
Invitations and announcements	Engraved	Engraved	Handwritten or telephoned invitations; engraved announcements
Decorations and accessories	Elaborate flowers for church, canopy to church, aisle carpet, pew ribbons, limousines for bridal party, groom's cake (given to guests in boxes), engraved matchbooks or napkins as mementos, rose petals or confetti	Flowers for church, aisle carpet, pew ribbons, rose petals (other items optional)	Flowers for altar, rose petals
Music	Organ at church (choir or soloist optional); orchestra for dancing at reception	Organ at church (choir or soloist optional); strolling musician, small orchestra, or records for reception; dancing optional	Organ at church; records at reception optional

Planning Your Wedding Ceremony

One of your first decisions will be the site for your wedding ceremony. When you have made your final choice, record all the pertinent information here.

Church or Synagogue: (Name) *Cedar Creek Community Church*
    Address:
    Telephone: *269-6204*
    Minister or rabbi's name and number: *Alex Dody*

Organist's name and number:

Date and time of wedding ceremony:

If you wish to write your own vows, have special passages read during the ceremony, or would like non-traditional music, be sure to discuss this with your priest or rabbi. Keep track of those passages you would like to include on page 70. Remember to take these with you when you meet with your minister or rabbi. Also, note any requirements you'll have to meet before the ceremony can take place.

    Appointments to see minister or rabbi:

    First Discussion appointment
        Date: Time:

    Counseling appointments
    1.   Date: Time:
    2.   Date: Time:
    3.   Date: Time:

    Special regulations or requirements:

    Documents: (Birth certificates, divorce papers, blood test, marriage
           license)
    1. _____

    2. _____

    3. _____

    4. _____

Checklist for first discussion with your minister or rabbi:

☐ Date, time and length of ceremony
  Number of guests church or synagogue will comfortably hold
☐ Whether your service will be traditional or whether you may write all or part of it yourselves
☐ Whether, when, and how photographs may be taken before, during and/or after the service
☐ Whether, when, and how videotaping may be conducted before, during and/or after the service
☐ If a second priest or rabbi will be participating, how arrangements should be made
☐ When to make appointment with organist to select music and/or whether you intend to have instrumental or vocal soloists
☐ What kind of floral arrangements/decorations are permitted; how to arrange access for the florist; the disposition of the flowers after the ceremony
☐ Whether there is a room for dressing prior to the service, if you require one
☐ If you should arrange for the services of a traffic officer
☐ Whether rice, rose petals, etc. are permitted to be thrown outside the building
☐ If you want an aisle carpet or runner, whether one is provided
☐ What fees are required for the use of the facility; the organist; for additional musicians; for the sexton; for the minister or rabbi

Be sure to make a reservation for the rehearsal at the time you make the reservation for your wedding ceremony. On page 64 you'll find room to list all those who should attend the rehearsal. Remember to notify the members of your bridal party about the day and time of the rehearsal. Make a check mark in the margin of the Bride's Checklist when you've done this.

Date and time of rehearsal:

Selecting your Caterer, Florist, Musicians, and Photographer

Unless you have a favorite in any of these categories already selected, you will want to shop around to be sure you are getting the best service for the best price. Use the following pages to make notes of what services each establishment offers and what the cost would be.

Initial questions to discuss with a caterer (whether at a reception site or one who will come to your home or other location) are:

- Is a wedding package offered?
- If so, what does it include and what does it cost?
- Are substitutions permissible?
- What food and drinks will be served at the cocktail hour? During the reception? Will brand name liquors or wines be served? If not, how much more would the cost be to serve them? Will there be an open bar for the cocktail hour? For the entire reception?
- What does a sample place setting consist of?
- Can you sample food and observe a party arranged by this caterer?
- Will the caterer provide printed directions to the catering hall for you to include with your invitations?
- Is insurance against china and crystal breakage included in the costs stated? If not, is it available and at what cost?
- What are the choices of table linen colors?
- Does the caterer work with a florist for centerpieces, and if so, does he have a book you may look at to select arrangements? If you prefer to provide your own decorations, how can that be arranged?
- May the reception be extended an extra hour? At what time do servers go on overtime pay? What is the cost of both options?
- Are all gratuities included in the stated costs?
- Is there a special rate for providing food and beverages for the musicians and photographers?

You should also discuss whether you'd prefer to have the caterer or another baker provide the wedding cake. Ask both the caterer and a bakery for a sample before deciding, to make sure it's to your liking. Ask both if there are photographs of wedding cakes they have provided in the past so you can select decorating style. Also discuss table arrangement—if you want a bridal table—how many guests the other tables seat comfortably—where speakers will be located if music will be amplified—whether you require a table for placecards.

Be sure to have all these details spelled out before signing a contract with your chosen caterer. Once you have decided on a caterer, remember to tell him or her about any details that are special to your wedding. For example, if you would like to use the knife your mother used to cut her wedding cake, arrange how to deliver it. If you plan to have a groom's cake, tell the caterer this, too.

Caterer

Name:
Address: Telephone:
Menus available:

Type of service (sit-down, buffet, etc.):

Help provided (waiters, bartenders, parking valet, etc.):

Wedding cake:

Tables and chairs:

Other services and equipment:

Price per person:
Additional costs:
Gratuities:
Estimated total:

Caterer

Name:
Address: Telephone:
Menus available:

Type of service (sit-down, buffet, etc.):

Help provided (waiters, bartenders, parking valet, etc.):

Wedding cake:

Tables and chairs:

Other services and equipment:

Price per person:
Additional costs:
Gratuities:
Estimated total:

Caterer

　　Name:
　　Address:　　　　　　　　　　　　　　　Telephone:
　　Menus available:

Type of service (sit-down, buffet, etc.):

Help provided (waiters, bartenders, parking valet, etc.):

Wedding cake:

Tables and chairs:

Other services and equipment:

　　Price per person:
　　Additional costs:
　　Gratuities:
　　Estimated total:

The Florist

Flowers add a lovely touch of color to any wedding. You'll want to make an appointment to speak with several florists to find one who'll add that perfect finishing touch of color to your wedding. Remember not to limit yourself to looking at catalogs of floral arrangements, ask to see samples of each florist's work.

Among the questions you might want to ask a florist are:

Does this florist offer a wedding package? What does it consist of? Is it possible to substitute different types of flowers for those in the package, and what are the costs involved?

Perhaps you prefer silk flowers. Does this florist handle them? If you choose silk flowers you might consider having your bridal bouquet made into a table centerpiece for your home. Could this florist do this for you?

What are this florist's delivery charges? If flowers are to be delivered to more than one location, the bride's home, church, and reception site for instance, what effect does this have on delivery charges?

Name:
Address:
Telephone:
Flowers for church:
   Description:
   Price:
Flowers for reception:
   Description:
   Price:
Bridesmaids' flowers:
   Description:
   Price:
Bride's bouquet:
   Description:
   Price:
Boutonnieres:
   Description:
   Price:
Corsages for mothers:
   Description:
   Price:
Others:
   Description:
   Price:
Services (delivery, removal, other):
Estimated total:

Name:

Address:

Telephone:

Flowers for church:
  Description:
  Price:

Flowers for reception:
  Description:
  Price:

Bridesmaids' flowers:
  Description:
  Price:

Bride's bouquet:
  Description:
  Price:

Boutonnieres:
  Description:
  Price:

Corsages for mothers:
  Description:
  Price:

Others:
  Description:
  Price:

Services (delivery, removal, other):

Estimated total:

Name:

Address:

Telephone:

Flowers for church:
  Description:
  Price:

Flowers for reception:
  Description:
  Price:

Bridesmaids' flowers:
  Description:
  Price:

Bride's bouquet:
  Description:
  Price:

Boutonnieres:
  Description:
  Price:

Corsages for mothers:
  Description:
  Price:

Others:
  Description:
  Price:

Services (delivery, removal, other):

Estimated total:

The Musicians

Shakespeare called music the food of love, and what an aura of romance the right music creates! When considering various orchestras remember to arrange to hear them play at a wedding or other social gathering rather than in a nightclub. You'll want to hear the different varieties of music the orchestra can provide for your wedding.

Name of orchestra:
Agent:
Address:

Telephone:

Number of pieces:
Instruments:

Length of playing time
   and rest periods:

Requirements: (chairs, piano,
   electrical needs, etc.)

Price:
Time and place to hear
   the orchestra play:

Comments:

Name of orchestra:
Agent:
Address:

Telephone:

Number of pieces:
Instruments:

Length of playing time
   and rest periods:

Requirements: (chairs, piano,
   electrical needs, etc.)

Price:
Time and place to hear
   the orchestra play:

Comments:

Name of orchestra:
Agent:
Address

Telephone:

Number of pieces:
Instruments:

Length of playing time
    and rest periods:

Requirements: (chairs, piano,
    electrical needs, etc.)

Price:
Time and place to hear
    the orchestra play:

Comments:

The Photographer

Visit several photo studios and study the quality of work each offers before deciding to whom you'll entrust the job of photographing your wedding. Be sure to study the samples of the photographer who'll actually photograph your wedding. Listed are some questions to help you compare photo packages, options, and prices before making your decision.

Name:
Address:
Telephone:

Does the photo studio offer a photo
    package?   _____

What does it consist of?   _____
What does it cost for additions to the
    package?   _____

What are the costs of
    Formal portraits of the bride: _____

    Formal portraits of bridal party: _____

What is the number of proofs taken at:
    The wedding?   _____

    The reception?   _____
What is the number of pages in the
    standard wedding album?   _____

    The cost?   _____

What does it cost per extra album page? _____

What is the size and cost of extra albums? _____

What is the cost of keeping all the proofs? _____
Will the photographer stay through the
    entire reception? or just through the
    cutting of the cake?   _____

Name:
Address:
Telephone:

————————————

————————————

————————————

————————————

————————————

————————————

————————————

————————————

————————————

————————————

————————————

Name:
Address:
Telephone:

————————————

————————————

————————————

————————————

————————————

————————————

————————————

————————————

————————————

————————————

————————————

The Videographer

Contact several video studios and make appointments to see videotapes of weddings they have covered before. Look carefully not only at the actual quality of the tape, but also at how it has been edited. Is the editing smooth or are there jumps and gaps? Is the sound clear? Does it cover the things you would want covered at your wedding? Listed are some questions to help you compare video options and prices before making your decision.

Name:

Address:

Telephone:

Does the video studio offer a wedding package? _____

What does it consist of? _____

What do additional copies cost? _____

Are there additional costs for:
videotaping the wedding party as a formal portrait? _____

restaging part of the ceremony if videotaping is not permitted during the actual ceremony? _____

Are there separate costs for taping the ceremony and the reception? _____

Will the videographer stay through the entire reception? or just through the cutting of the cake? _____

Name: Name:
Address: Address:
Telephone: Telephone:

_____   _____

_____   _____

_____   _____

_____   _____

_____   _____

_____   _____

_____   _____

Dress for Bridal Party and Guests

The clothing selected by the bridal party and guests is determined by the formality of the ceremony. Use this chart to guide you in your selections.

	Most Formal Daytime	*Most Formal Evening*	*Semiformal Daytime*
Bride	Long white dress, train, and veil; gloves optional	Same as most formal daytime	Long white dress; short veil and gloves optional
Bride's attendants	Long dresses, matching shoes; gloves are bride's option	Same as most formal daytime	Same as most formal daytime
Groom, his attendants, bride's father, or stepfather	Cutaway coat, striped trousers, pearl gray waistcoat, white stiff shirt, turndown collar with gray-and-black-striped four-in-hand or wing collar with ascot, gray gloves, black silk socks, black kid shoes	Black tailcoat and trousers, white pique waistcoat, starched-bosom shirt, wing collar, white bow tie, white gloves, black silk socks, black patent-leather shoes or pumps or black kid smooth-toe shoes	Black or charcoal sack coat, dove gray waistcoat, white pleated shirt, starched turndown collar or soft white shirt with four-in-hand tie, gray gloves, black smooth-toe shoes
Mothers, and stepmothers, of couple	Long or short dresses; hat, veil, or hair ornament; gloves	Usually long evening or dinner dress, dressy short cocktail permissible; veil or hair ornament if long dress; small hat, if short; gloves	Long or street-length dresses, gloves; head covering optional
Women guests	Street-length cocktail or afternoon dresses (colors are preferable to black or white); gloves; head covering optional	Depending on local custom, long or short dresses; if long, veil or ornament— otherwise, hat optional; gloves	Short afternoon or cocktail dress; head covering for church optional
Men guests	Dark suits; conservative shirts and ties	If women wear long dresses, tuxedos; if short dresses, dark suits	Dark suits

	Semiformal Evening	Informal Daytime	Informal Evening
Bride	Same as semiformal daytime	Short afternoon dress, cocktail dress, or suit	Long dinner dress or short cocktail dress or suit
Bride's attendants	Same length and degree of formality as bride's dress	Same style as bride	Same style as bride
Groom, his attendants, bride's father, or stepfather	Winter, black tuxedo; summer, white jacket; pleated or piqué soft shirt, black cummerbund, black bow tie, no gloves, black patent-leather or kid shoes	Winter, dark suit; summer, dark trousers with white linen jacket or white trousers with navy or charcoal jacket; soft shirt, conservative four-in-hand tie; hot climate, white suit	Tuxedo if bride wears dinner dress; dark suit in winter, lighter suit in summer
Mothers and stepmothers of couple	Same as semiformal daytime	Short afternoon or cocktail dresses	Same length dress as bride
Women guests	Cocktail dresses, gloves; head covering for church optional	Afternoon dresses, gloves; head covering for church optional	Afternoon or cocktail dresses, gloves; head covering for church optional
Men guests	Dark suits	Dark suits; light trousers and dark blazers in summer	Dark suits
Groom's father, or stepfather	He may wear the same costume as the groom and his attendants, especially if he is to stand in the receiving line. If he is not to take part, however, and does not wish to dress formally, he may wear the same clothes as the men guests.		

Clothes for Your Bridal Party

Your first shopping trip for your gown should be an investigative one. There is no need to exceed your budget; include bridal shops, dressmakers, evening wear departments of stores, and the relatively new formal rental shops for women in your first considerations. The type of wedding you have chosen—formal, semiformal or informal—should be your guide to what you select to wear.

When you select your bridesmaids' dresses, consider their finances, too. Try to choose dresses that can be worn again, either as is, or with simple alterations.

Bride's Attire
   Store:
   Address: Telephone:
   Description (color, material, style, etc.):

   Salesperson:
   Date ordered:
   Fitting appointments:

To ensure a perfect fit, be sure to wear the undergarments and shoes you'll wear for the wedding when you go for your fittings.

   Pick-up time:

Accessories
   Shoes:
   Headdress:
   Jewelry:
   Other:

Notes

As soon as she selects her dress, the mother of the bride should let the mother of the groom know what style and color she has chosen. The mother of the groom can then pick out a complementary dress. If the bride or groom has a stepmother, the bride should be the one to let the stepmother(s) know what the natural mothers are wearing so that they are able to select dresses complimentary but not similar to the natural mother's dress. Record their choices below.

Mother of the Bride
    Store:
    Address: Telephone:
    Description:
    Salesperson:
    Fitting appointment:
    Pick-up date:
    Accessories:

Mother of the Groom
    Store:
    Address: Telephone:
    Description:
    Salesperson:
    Fitting appointment:
    Pick-up date:
    Accessories:

Fathers of the Bride and Groom

Since he will escort his daughter down the aisle, the father of the bride will wear the same style clothing as the groom and his attendants. The father of the groom may wear the same clothing as his son and his son's attendants, and should do so if he will stand in the receiving line.

Attendants' Dresses
  Store:
  Address: Telephone:
  Description:
  Salesperson:

  Accessories:

  Ordered on:
  Will be ready for fittings by:
  Delivery date:

SIZES

Attendant's Name	Dress	Shoe

If possible, get samples of dress material to help in selecting flowers and having shoes dyed. Attendants who live nearby should make their own appointments for fittings. Dresses should be mailed to others in time for them to have any necessary alterations made. If you've decided to have a flower girl in your bridal party be sure to include her here, and don't forget to inform her parents when her dress will be ready too.

Groom and Ushers

The groom, his best man, and the ushers will wear identical outfits, except that the groom may select an ascot or tie in a different pattern. The clothes are almost always rented, and should be ordered from the same rental agency so that they will match. Ask out-of-town ushers to send their sizes and measurements well in advance so that the groom can reserve their outfits for them.

Store:
Address: Telephone:
Description

Salesperson:

Ordered on: Ushers may go in for fittings on:
Pick-up and return times:

SIZES

Name	Regular Size	Waist	Trouser Length	Collar	Sleeve Length	Shoe

If you're having a ring bearer in your bridal party include him here and don't forget to inform his parents when his clothing will be ready too.

The Traditional Division of Expenses

The division of expenses listed below is the traditional one and there are, of course, many variations. Today the bride and groom often pay their own wedding costs, particularly when the wedding is a second one for either or both. The groom's family often offers to pay a share and it is quite acceptable for the bride's parents to accept this offer, especially if the groom and his family would like a larger or more elaborate reception than the bride's parents can afford. Use these pages as a guide, and make your own adjustments.

Expenses of the Bride and Her Family

- Services of a bridal consultant and/or a secretary
- Invitations, announcements, and enclosures
- The bride's wedding dress and accessories
- Floral decorations for ceremony and reception, bridesmaids' flowers, bride's bouquet (in some areas given by groom)
- Formal wedding photographs and candid pictures
- Videotape recording of wedding
- Music for church and reception
- Transportation of bridal party to ceremony, and from ceremony to reception, if hired cars are used
- All expenses of reception
- Bride's presents to her attendants
- Bride's present to groom, if she wishes to give him one
- The groom's wedding ring, if it is to be a double-ring ceremony
- Rental of awning for ceremony entrance and carpet for aisle, if desired and if not provided by church
- Fee for services performed by sexton
- A traffic officer, if necessary
- Transportation and lodging expenses for priest or rabbi if from another town and if invited to officiate by bride's family
- Accommodations for bride's attendants, if required
- Bridesmaid's luncheon, if one is given by the bride

Expenses of the Groom and His Family

- Bride's engagement and wedding rings
- Groom's present to his bride, if he wishes to give her one
- Gifts for the groom's attendants
- Accommodations for groom's attendants, if required
- Boutonnieres for the groom's attendants
- Ties and gloves for the groom's attendants, if not part of their clothing rental package
- The bride's bouquet in areas where local custom requires it
- The bride's going-away corsage
- Corsages for immediate members of both families (unless bride has included them in her florist's order)
- The minister's or rabbi's fee or donation
- Transportation and lodging expenses for minister or rabbi if from another town and if invited to officiate by the groom's family
- The marriage license
- Transportation for the groom and best man to the ceremony
- Expenses of the honeymoon
- All costs of the rehearsal dinner, if one is held
- Bachelor dinner, if groom wishes to give one
- Transportation and lodging expenses for groom's parents

Bridal Party Expenses

Bridesmaid's/honor attendant's expenses

- Purchase of apparel and all accessories
- Transportation to and from the city or town where the wedding takes place
- A contribution to a gift from all the bridesmaids to the bride
- An individual gift to the couple
- A shower and/or luncheon for the bride

Usher's/Best man's expenses

- Rental of wedding attire
- Transportation to and from location of wedding
- A contribution to a gift from all the groom's attendants to the groom
- An individual gift to the couple
- A bachelor dinner, if given by the groom's attendants

Budget Planner

Following is a sample budget for a semiformal wedding with 100 guests, 4 attendants, and a reception held in a club or catered at home to help you plan your own budget. Many of these costs may be considerably more or less, depending on where you live and how elaborate or simple your plans are. For example, a friend who bakes beautifully may want to give your wedding cake as a gift, or you may wear your mother's wedding gown which would require only simple alterations and cleaning. Music for your reception may be tapes you make yourselves and have played over a music system, or it may be a three- or more piece band.

Other areas of savings would be to have attendants stay at your homes or at the homes of friends, forgoing a professional videographer, having a picnic rehearsal dinner rather than one in a restaurant or club, and skipping a bridesmaid's luncheon and bachelor's dinner.

The reception costs vary greatly across the country, and with the type of reception you plan. A buffet brunch is less expensive than a seated dinner, for example, and a cocktails and hors d'oeuvres plus wedding cake reception can be not only lovely but also comparatively inexpensive.

The best way to plan is to begin with your fixed costs, such as the priest's or rabbi's fee and organist's fee, the cost for the sexton or facility for the ceremony, gifts for your attendants, postage, the marriage license fee and your wedding rings. Subtract that total from your available funds and see what amount you have to work with. This will give you a guide as to how much you have left for variable costs, such as limousines, a photographer, and the rehearsal dinner and reception.

Following the sample budget are pages for you to enter your own budget information. In the first column, enter the projected amounts, and then as costs are confirmed or paid, enter the actual amount spent.

Sample Budget

Bride's gown	$400
Bride's accessories	100
Invitations/enclosures	150
Announcements	75
Postage	50
Flowers for ceremony	80
Flowers for reception	250
Bride's bouquet	50
Flowers for bride's attendants	120
Corsages	40
Boutonnieres	50
Organist's fee	75
Cantor/vocalist/instrumentalist fee	50
Music for reception	850
Sexton's/facility fee	25
Minister's or Rabbi's fee	100
Limousines for bridal party	200
Photographer	500
Videographer	800
Bride's gifts for attendants	125
Groom's gifts for attendants	125
Bride's ring	100
Groom's ring	100
Marriage license	20
Accommodations for bride's attendants	400
Accommodations for groom's attendants	400
Rehearsal dinner—$30 per person	500
Bridesmaid's luncheon	50
Bachelor's dinner	200
Reception expenses—$50 per person	5,500
Wedding cake	100
	$11,585

Your Budget

Enter the amount you think you will spend on each item in the second column and the amount you actually spend in the third.

Item	Projected Amount	Amount Spent
Bride's gown		
Bride's accessories		
Invitations/enclosures		
Announcements		
Postage		
Flowers for ceremony		
Flowers for reception		
Bride's bouquet		
Flowers for bride's attendants		
Corsages		
Boutonnieres		
Organist's fee		
Cantor/vocalist/instrumentalist fee		
Sexton's/facility fee		
Minister's or Rabbi's fee		
Limousines for bridal party		
Photographer		
Videographer		
Bride's gifts for attendants		
Groom's gifts for attendants		
Bride's ring		
Groom's ring		

Item	Projected Amount	Amount Spent
Marriage license		
Blood test (where required)		
Accommodations for bride's attendants		
Accommodations for groom's attendants		
Rehearsal dinner		
Food		
Beverages		
Reception expenses		
Food		
Beverages		
Premises usage fee		
Incidentals		
Gratuities		
Music		
Wedding cake		

Out-of-Town Guest's Accommodations

Guests who come from a distance pay their own travel and lodging expenses. The parents of the bride or groom should assist their relatives and friends by making reservations, and may offer to pay any expenses they wish to assume, but are not at all required to do so. They may also accept the offers of local friends and relatives to provide accommodations for out-of-town guests in their homes.

Reservations Made For	Dates	Name and Address of Hotel or Motel	Telephone

Invitations, Announcements and Guest List

Your invitations set the tone of your wedding. If you are having an elegant, formal wedding, your invitations should be elegant and formal, too. The most formal invitation is the traditional one with the wording all in the third person. A more personally-worded invitation is appropriate as well. The options are yours, and the best way to begin is to consult your stationer and look at his or her sample books for ideas. Remember, though, that the simplest invitations, without frills and adornments, are in the best taste.

Stationers
    Name:
    Address and Telephone:
    Invitations
        Quantity:
        Design # Chosen:
        Estimate:
    Reception Invitation
        Quantity:
        Design # Chosen:
        Estimate:
    Response Card
        Quantity:
        Design # Chosen:
        Estimate:
    Pew Card
        Quantity:
        Design # Chosen:
        Estimate:
    Announcements
        Quantity:
        Design # Chosen:
        Estimate:
    At Home Cards
        Quantity:
        Design # Chosen:
        Estimate:

Name:

Address and Telephone:

Invitations

    Quantity:

    Design # Chosen:

    Estimate:

Reception Invitation

    Quantity:

    Design # Chosen:

    Estimate:

Response Card

    Quantity:

    Design # Chosen:

    Estimate:

Pew Card

    Quantity:

    Design # Chosen:

    Estimate:

Announcements

    Quantity:

    Design # Chosen:

    Estimate:

At Home Cards

    Quantity:

    Design # Chosen:

    Estimate:

Place a check mark in the margin next to the stationer you've selected. Make a note of the day you placed your order, and the day it is to be ready.

If you wish to have printed favors for your reception, such as cocktail napkins, check with your stationer to see if he or she is able to provide them, as well. If not, look in the yellow pages of your telephone directory for specialty printers. You might check whether the favors you want are available in one of the colors you've selected for your bridal party.

Matchbooks
> folding or box

with printed monogram and the date
> quantity and cost:

with printed names and the date
> quantity and cost:

Cocktail Napkins

with a monogram and the date
> quantity and cost:

with your names and the date
> quantity and cost:

If you decide to order favors be sure to note when they'll be ready (if the date is different from the date your invitations and announcements will be ready).

Many wedding ceremonies and/or receptions end with the guests showering the bride and groom with a cascade of rice or paper rose petals. If you have decided to include one of these options in your wedding, after checking with your priest or rabbi or reception site manager to make sure this is permissible, see if the rose petals can be ordered from your stationer. Another very nice option, especially for an outdoor wedding, is to use birdseed instead.

Use this page to decide on the exact wording of your wedding invitation. Make sure you take a copy with you when you visit stationers.

Date and time invitations are to be picked up:

Use this page to determine the wording of your wedding announcement, if you'll be sending announcements. The announcements should be ordered at the same time as the invitations.

Date and time announcements are to be picked up:

Guest List

This list provides a quick, at-a-glance reference. You can also keep an indexed file with each guest's name and address on an individual card.

_____ _____

_____ _____

_____ _____

_____ _____

_____ _____

_____ _____

_____ _____

_____ _____

_____ _____

_____ _____

_____ _____

_____ _____

_____ _____

_____ _____

_____ _____

_____ _____

Guest List

_____   _____

_____   _____

_____   _____

_____   _____

_____   _____

_____   _____

_____   _____

_____   _____

_____   _____

_____   _____

_____   _____

_____   _____

_____   _____

_____   _____

_____   _____

_____   _____

_____   _____

Guest List

_____   _____

_____   _____

_____   _____

_____   _____

_____   _____

_____   _____

_____   _____

_____   _____

_____   _____

_____   _____

_____   _____

_____   _____

_____   _____

_____   _____

_____   _____

_____   _____

_____   _____

Guest List

Guest List

_____   _____

_____   _____

_____   _____

_____   _____

_____   _____

_____   _____

_____   _____

_____   _____

_____   _____

_____   _____

_____   _____

_____   _____

_____   _____

_____   _____

_____   _____

_____   _____

_____   _____

Showers and Parties

In the midst of all the fun and excitement of planning your wedding, you will want to keep track of the wonderful showers and parties given in your honor. Use these pages to record the names and addresses of those friends and relatives who attended these parties. You can also use these lists to send thank-you notes to those you're unable to thank in person.

Type of shower:
    Hostess/Host:
    Date and time:
    Location: Telephone:

GUESTS

Name	*Address*

Type of shower:
  Hostess/Host:
  Date and time:
  Location: Telephone:

GUESTS

Name   *Address*

_____

_____

_____

_____

_____

_____

_____

_____

_____

_____

_____

_____

_____

_____

_____

_____

_____

_____

_____

_____

_____

Other Parties Honoring the Bride and Groom

    Kind of party (luncheon, cocktail, etc.):
    Hostess/Host:
    Place:
    Date and time:

GUESTS

Name	**Address**

Kind of party (luncheon, cocktail, etc.):
Hostess/Host:
Place:
Date and time:

GUESTS

Name	Address

Your Wedding Rehearsal

As much fun as all the parties and activities that surround your wedding are, it is important to keep in mind that what they are celebrating is your marriage. The ceremony is really the focus of these events, and the two of you and your attendants should take the rehearsal seriously, arriving on time and nicely dressed.

You will have discussed all the details of your ceremony ahead of time with your minister or rabbi, and he or she is the one in charge of the rehearsal. He or she will not necessarily go through the whole service, but may go through several sections more than once to be sure everything goes smoothly.

In addition to practicing the processional and the recessional and going through the service, the ushers should be briefed by you on who will sit in the reserved pews, and instructed as to how people should be seated in the other pews. For example, they should be alerted to the traditional bride's side (left) and groom's side (right) and whether you wish them to balance seating if one side has many more guests than the other, or if either the bride's or the groom's parents are divorced, which should be seated to the front and which behind that parent and his or her family members.

This is also the time to decide which ushers will roll out the carpet and put the ribbons on the ends of the pews, who will escort the mothers, etc.

It is also a good idea to instruct ushers on the manner in which they are to escort guests—how to offer an arm, whether to precede guests to their seats, etc.

Your priest or rabbi should instruct the bridesmaids on how to pace themselves during the processional so that they walk neither too fast nor too slow. If you think it is necessary, you may ask another friend or relative to be present who can assist with this during the actual ceremony.

The bride should carry a paper bouquet or something resembling what she will carry during the ceremony so that she and the maid of honor can get used to how they will transfer her bouquet at the beginning and the end of the ceremony.

If special music is to be played, poems to be read, or nontraditional vows said, these should be practiced at the rehearsal so that they will be performed easily and naturally during the ceremony itself.

The mothers of the flower girl and ring bearer should attend the rehearsal with their children, if possible, so that they know what the expectations will be during the ceremony.

The groom's parents may be invited to attend, but their presence is not necessary since they have no active part in the ceremony and if they are hosting the rehearsal dinner, they may prefer to be attending to last-minute arrangements for the dinner, instead. In order that they not feel left out, however, the two of you should extend an invitation to them but give them the option of not attending if that is what they wish.

If a guest book will be used at the ceremony, the rehearsal is the time to make sure it is in place and that the person attending it (an usher or a family member) is instructed on what to do.

Make notes of any special instructions or arrangements on page 69.

People Present at Rehearsal

List attendants and check off as they are notified of time, date and other details.

Bride's attendants   Groom's attendants

_____   _____

_____   _____

_____   _____

_____   _____

_____   _____

_____   _____

_____   _____

_____   _____

Mother of the Bride: Bride's Escort:
Clergyperson:
Organist: Soloist:
Others:

During your rehearsal, you will practice the processional and recessional. Illustrated on the facing page are the traditional formations for both.

Traditional Formation for the Processional
and the Recessional

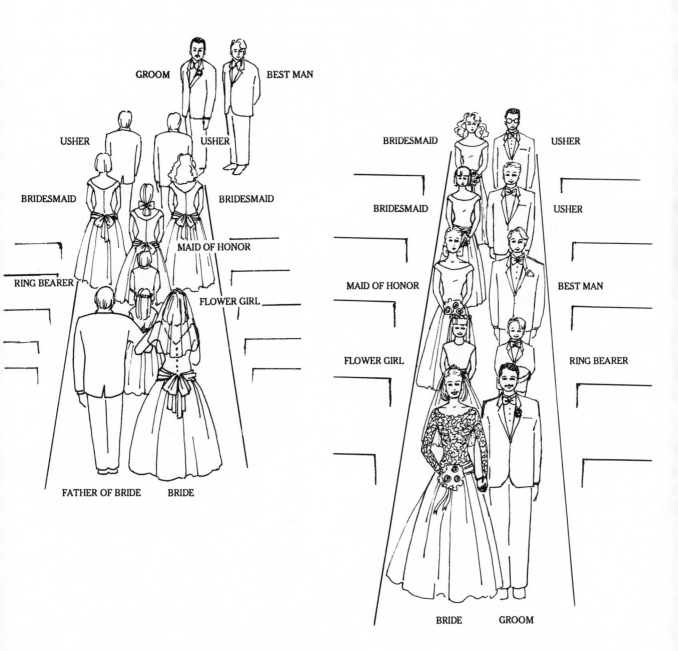

Rehearsal Dinner

Although the groom's family usually gives the rehearsal dinner, you may be able to help by assisting with the guest list, and, if they come from out of town, by reserving a place and making many of the arrangements.

Name (club, hotel, restaurant):
Name of manager:
Address: Telephone:

Menu:

Beverages:

Music or entertainment:

Guests

_____   _____   _____

_____   _____   _____

_____   _____   _____

_____   _____   _____

_____   _____   _____

_____   _____   _____

_____   _____   _____

The Ceremony

Flowers for Church

Altar arrangements:
  Description:
  Price:

Ends of pews:
  Description:
  Price:

Others:
  Description:
  Price:

Others:
  Description:
  Price:

Notes:

Music for Ceremony

Organ selections preceding ceremony:_____

_____

_____

_____

Processional selection:_____

Recessional selection:_____

Soloist
  Name:
  Address and telephone:
  Selections:

Organist's fee:
Soloist's fee (if professional):

Suggested Selections:

Music for the ceremony should be joyous and meaningful, but "popular" music is not acceptable in many churches and synagogues. Traditional love songs—such as "I Love You Truly" or "Oh Promise Me" may be played in some churches, but not in others. The traditional wedding march is out of favor, but still means "Here Comes the Bride" to me. Your organist will help you choose music that is fitting and suits your taste.

Reserved Pews

Several pews in the front of the church may be reserved for relatives and close friends of the bride and groom. If you choose to send out reserved pew cards, those holding them should bring them to the church and show them to the usher escorting them. At a small wedding where the ushers know all the guests, cards are not always sent and the ushers are told which guests are to be seated "within the ribbons."

Bride's guests seated in reserved pews
Pew 1. Parents of the bride

Pew 2.

Pew 3.

Pew 4.

Pew 5.

Pew 6.

Groom's guests seated in reserved pews
Pew 1. Parents of the groom

Pew 2.

Pew 3.

Pew 4.

Pew 5.

Pew 6.

Special Notes

Head usher:

Usher to escort mother of the bride:

Usher to escort grandmother of the bride:

Usher to escort mother of the groom:

Usher to escort grandmother of the groom:

Ushers to roll out aisle runner, if used:

Usher or attendant to pass out rice, rose petals or birdseed, if permitted, at ceremony site:

If the bride's parents are divorced, where will mother (and stepfather) sit? Father and stepmother?

If the groom's parents are divorced, where will mother (and stepfather) sit? Father and stepmother?

Person escorting the bride?

(She may walk alone or be escorted by anyone of her choosing if her father is estranged or deceased.)

Persons reading special poem or verses:

Persons lighting candles, if used:

Person in charge of guest book, if at ceremony instead of reception:

Notes on other special situations:

You may choose to make your wedding ceremony extra special by including a favorite passage or poem to be read during service or even by writing your own vows. Jot down your thoughts here and be sure to discuss these with your minister or rabbi.

_____

_____

_____

_____

_____

_____

_____

Guests' responses (to be printed and passed out as guests enter church)

_____

_____

_____

_____

_____

_____

_____

Your Reception

Use this page to keep track of the arrangements made with your caterer. Be sure to transfer his or her name to page 8.

Name:

Address:

Telephone:

Estimate:

Price per guest.................................... $

Bar price, if separate .... $

Gratuities .... $

Extras .... $

Number of guests:

Total price...................................... $

Number of serving staff:

Tables rented (number and price, if not from caterer):
Tent, awning, etc. (size and price, if not from caterer):

Number and shape of tables:

Number of chairs at tables:

Where rented (if not from caterer):
    Price:

Notes:

_____

_____

_____

_____

_____

_____

Menu

Hors d'oeuvres (if cocktail hour or if cocktail reception only):
type and amount:
1.
2.
3.
4.
5.

Beverages during cocktail hour (open bar, punch, champagne, etc):

Appetizer (if seated meal):

Entreé (if seated):

Entreé choices (if buffet):
1.
2.
3.

Salad:

Breads:

Condiments:

Beverages during meal:

Dessert:

Coffee (caffeinated, decaffeinated) and tea:

Wedding Cake

Where ordered:
Name of salesperson:
Description:

Price:

Time of delivery:

Placement of table for cake:

Floral Arrangements or Centerpieces

Number of centerpieces required:

    Color and style:

    If ordered from other than caterer
        Time for delivery:
        Person responsible for receiving them:
        Name of florist:

Table linens

    Tablecloth color:
        Fabric type:

    Napkin color:
        Fabric type:

Groom's Cake

Fruit cake cut in tiny squares and packaged in white boxes or paper to be taken home by your guests, for good luck, is called a groom's cake. It can be expensive if ordered from a bakery or caterer, but a friend might bake the cake and package it as a wedding gift.

    Provided by: Price:

Another kind of groom's cake can be a chocolate cake which is not cut by the bride and groom, but which is served at the reception as an addition or option to the regular wedding cake.

    Where ordered:
    Price:
    Delivery time:

Receiving Line

A receiving line may be formed either at the end of the ceremony or at the beginning of the reception. Whether you want the bride's attendants in the receiving line or not is entirely up to the two of you. Personally, I feel that it makes the line unnecessarily long, but this is something you two should decide together. Fathers in the receiving line are optional, but if one is in the line, the other should be, too. If either the bride's or the groom's parents are divorced, they should not stand in the line together.

If the bride's father and stepmother are hosting the reception, her stepmother, not her natural mother, would stand in the receiving line. If the bride's father and stepmother and mother and stepfather are hosting the wedding together, both her stepmother and mother may be in the line, but they should be separated by the groom's mother. The groom's mother or stepmother may stand in the line, depending on which he lived with when growing up. If his parents divorced after he was grown and his father remarried later, only the groom's mother would stand in the line.

Order of line

Mother of the bride, (Father of the bride, optional), Mother of the groom, (Father of the groom, optional), Bride, Groom, Maid of honor, Bridesmaid, Bridesmaid, Bridesmaid, Bridesmaid

MOTHER OF BRIDE   MOTHER OF GROOM   BRIDE   GROOM   MAID OF HONOR   BRIDESMAID   BRIDESMAID

FATHER OF BRIDE   FATHER OF GROOM
(OPTIONAL)   (OPTIONAL)

RECEIVING LINE

Guest Register

If a guest register is used, it is located at the site of the ceremony when more guests are invited to the wedding than to the reception. Otherwise, it is placed near the entrance to the reception and you may select several friends to tend it and see that everyone who enters signs it. These friends, as well as special friends who may be asked to help serve punch or cut and serve cake at a home wedding, are often known as "hostesses." Make a list of these friends and try to arrange a schedule that divides the time each serves equally.

Hostesses

_____   _____
_____   _____
_____   _____

Bridal Table

In addition to the bridal party, spouses, live-in companions and fiancés of the attendants should be seated at the bridal table, if room permits. If it doesn't, care should be taken to seat them near the bridal table and with congenial people.

If you will be using placecards for the bridal table, obtain them ahead of time, inscribe them and have a friend set them at their proper places before the reception or draw a diagram so that the caterer can put them in place for you. List your bridal table placecard names here.

Parents' Table

I have always felt it is in the true spirit of joining together to have the parents of the bride and groom sit together during the reception. In this case, grandparents, godparents, and the minister or rabbi and his or her spouse would share this table. Often, however, the bride's parents host at one table and the groom's parents at another, with respective grandparents and other relatives with them.

If either set of parents is divorced, separate parents' tables must be set so that the divorced pair need not sit together, but each may sit apart with his or her own family and friends.

Guest Tables

Obviously, if a full meal is to be served, there must be seating for all guests. But even at a buffet reception, there should be enough tables so that guests can find a place to sit down and enjoy their food and drinks.

You may plan tables and prepare placecards for guest tables, or you may leave it to their choice. If you do arrange groupings, be sure to try to seat people at tables where they know at least one other person. I also feel strongly that there should not be a bride's side of the room and a groom's side of the room. Although there are traditional "sides" during the ceremony, the reception is the party which brings everyone together. Intermingle complete tables of friends of the groom's family and friend's of the bride's family around the room. There should be no line of demarcation here.

Photographs

Give the photographer a list of people you want included in formal photographs taken of bridal party at start of reception.

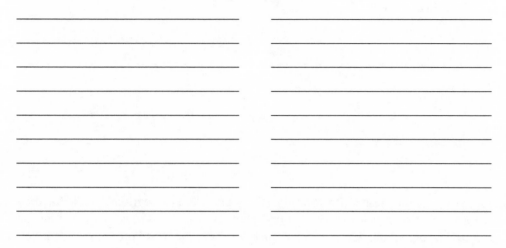

List of relatives and friends you want to be sure appear in candid photographs. Make a copy of this list and ask a close friend to point out these people to the photographer.

Musical Selections for Reception

Whether you have a strolling guitarist, a ten-piece orchestra, or music on a stereo tape deck, you will want certain personal favorites played. List them here as you think of them.

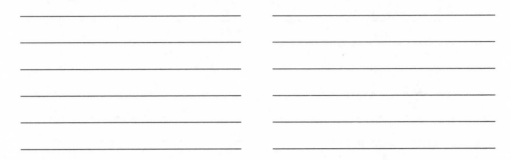

Go over your selections with your musicians, and ask a close friend to see that they have a list of them when the reception starts. If your music will be provided by a stereo or tape deck, arrange *in advance* for the selections you want played. You might also ask a friend to keep an eye on the music to see that continual music is played, if that's what you wish.

Using a Bridal Registry

Many of your relatives and friends will want to know what you would like as a gift. The best way to help them choose, and to assure yourself that you will receive gifts that you want and need, is to register your choices at those stores that have bridal registries in your community. When you list your choices in the stores try to select open patterns of china and crystal—patterns that will be available in the future if you wish to add to what you receive now.

When you register, be sure to pick items in various price ranges to accommodate the budgets of all your friends.

Some people object to the bridal registry as being too impersonal and commercial but I personally think it is an invaluable help to both bride and donor.

Second-time brides may also use a bridal registry. Although gifts are not required for a second wedding, those close to the bride and groom almost always want to give a gift, and particularly need shopping suggestions, believing that the bride may already have everything she wants or needs. In this situation, registering your "wish list" is especially helpful.

Do not register for the same gifts at different stores or you will surely receive many duplicates. Bridal registry personnel remove an item from your list once it has been purchased for you so that more than one person does not buy it. They have no way of knowing what has been bought at another store, however, since they naturally do not cross-reference with one another.

If the groom comes from another town, his friends and relatives are at a disadvantage if they cannot easily get to stores in your area, where you have registered. Talk to the groom's mother about what stores are located in her town or city. If there is a branch of the same store as is in your town, the bridal registry for your store will cross-reference with the other store if you notify them to do so. If there are no stores common to both towns, see if the groom's mother can obtain store catalogs for you to mark selections and return to her. She, then, can register for you at those stores.

Pattern Selections

Note here the patterns you select for tableware.

Fine china: _____

Casual dinnerware: _____

Crystal: _____

Sterling flatware: _____

Stainless flatware: _____

Stores Where Gifts are Registered

Name: _____

Address: _____   Telephone: _____

Registrar: _____

Name: _____

Address: _____   Telephone: _____

Registrar: _____

Name: _____

Address: _____   Telephone: _____

Registrar: _____

Name: _____

Address: _____   Telephone: _____

Registrar: _____

Gifts

Gift List

In order to keep your gifts organized, to know who gave what and where it came from in case of exchanges, and whether or not a thank-you has been sent, it is essential to keep an orderly gift list. You can get sheets of numbered stickers (or plain ones on which you can write a number) and affix one sticker in the correct column here and one with a corresponding number on the bottom of the gift. If you do this faithfully as the gifts arrive, there will be no possibility of confusion.

Gift No.	Description	Donor	Where Purchased	Date Rec'd	Thank You
0	Wooden salad bowl	Mr. & Mrs. Wm. Tell	Bloomingdale's	8/16	8/18

Gift No.	Description	Donor	Where Purchased	Date Rec'd	Thank You

Gift No.	Description	Donor	Where Purchased	Date Rec'd	Thank You

Gift No.	Description	Donor	Where Purchased	Date Rec'd	Thank You

Gift No.	Description	Donor	Where Purchased	Date Rec'd	Thank You

Gift No.	Description	Donor	Where Purchased	Date Rec'd	Thank You

Gift No.	Description	Donor	Where Purchased	Date Rec'd	Thank You

Gift No.	Description	Donor	Where Purchased	Date Rec'd	Thank You

Gift No.	Description	Donor	Where Purchased	Date Rec'd	Thank You

Gift No.	Description	Donor	Where Purchased	Date Rec'd	Thank You

Exchanges and Replacements

Problems sometimes arise when gifts are delivered. Keep notes on exchanges, breakage, duplicate gifts you plan to exchange.

Exchanges

    Item exchanged:
    Replacement chosen: Donor:
    Store:

    Item exchanged:
    Replacement chosen: Donor:
    Store:

    Item exchanged:
    Replacement chosen: Donor:
    Store:

Breakage
    Item broken:
    Store where purchased: Donor:

    Item broken:
    Store where purchased: Donor:

Duplicates and Other Problems:

Gifts for Attendants

While the two of you have been the recipients of many lovely gifts you should attempt to bestow upon those family and friends who served in your bridal party a gift that expresses your true feelings toward them as well as your gratitude.

The bride often gives her attendants a piece of jewelry which they can wear during the wedding, such as a necklace, a bracelet, or earrings. Usually the maid and/or matron of honor are given a gift which is slightly different from those given to the bridesmaids, simply because of their positions of honor and because their responsibilities are greater. For example, if you select earrings as a gift for your attendants, the honor attendant's might be a cluster of pearls and the others' a single pearl.

Junior bridesmaids' gifts may be the same as the other bridesmaids, if appropriate for their ages, or may be something different, if not appropriate. The flower girl's gift may also be jewelry—a special memento of her first wedding could be, for example, a small bracelet engraved with her initials and your wedding date. Another gift, also appropriate for a ring bearer, would be a music box, special box for keeping treasures with their names on them, or a wonderful book with an inscription written by you.

Groom's gifts to his attendants can also be jewelry, or dresser or travel accessories, as examples. Any of these may be engraved, if you wish, with the recipient's initials. As is true for the maid and/or matron of honor, the best man's gift is usually slightly different from those given to the ushers.

The bride and groom generally give their gifts at the bridesmaids' luncheon and bachelor's dinner, if held. If these events are not held, the gifts would be given at the rehearsal dinner or, in the absence of a rehearsal dinner, directly following the rehearsal for the ceremony.

Attendants Gift Record

Record here the specifics for the gifts you order for your attendants. Be sure to order anything that has to be personalized or engraved well in advance to ensure that it will be ready in time to give your attendants before your wedding ceremony.

Maid of honor's gift:
    Store: Salesperson:
    Date ordered: Delivery date: Price:

Matron of honor's gift:
    Store: Salesperson:
    Date ordered: Delivery date: Price:

Bridesmaids' gifts:
    Store: Salesperson:
    Date ordered: Delivery date: Price:

Flower girl's gift:
    Store: Salesperson:
    Date ordered: Delivery date: Price:

Ring Bearer's gift:
    Store: Salesperson:
    Date ordered: Delivery date: Price:

Best man's gift:
    Store: Salesperson:
    Date ordered: Delivery date: Price:

Ushers' gifts:
    Store: Salesperson:
    Date ordered: Delivery date: Price:

The Newspaper Announcement

If you want your wedding to be announced in the newspapers, you will be expected to provide the newspaper with the necessary information, and also a photograph, if you wish. Large city newspapers have their own forms which they will send you at your request. Smaller newspapers will want your notice sent to them at least ten days or two weeks in advance and the sooner you do so, the more certain you can be that your announcement will appear. Newspapers only print as many announcements as space permits. They may rework your wording or may eliminate some of the information you send. Send the information to the Society Editor—if there is none it will be forwarded to the correct department. Make sure to include a release date and also a daytime phone number where either of you can be reached in case the newspaper seeks to verify any information.

Newspaper announcement will be sent to:

Name of newspaper:
Address:

Name of newspaper:
Address:

Name of newspaper:
Address:

    It is also courteous to ask the mother of the groom whether she would like the announcement sent to her local papers. Or, she may send the announcement in herself if she has personal contacts at the newspaper.

    Before writing your own wedding announcement, read those in your local paper. Select the wording you like best, and if you are lucky, yours will be printed in just that way.

Information That Should be Included in the Announcement

Bride's full name

Bride's parents' name and address

Bride's parents' occupations

Bride's maternal and paternal grandparents

Bride's school and college

Bride's occupation

Groom's full name and address

Groom's parents' name and address

Groom's parents' occupations

Groom's maternal and paternal grandparents

Groom's school and college

Groom's occupation

Date of wedding

Location of wedding and reception

Names of bride's attendants (relation-
ship to bride or groom)

Names of groom's attendants (rela-
tionship to bride or groom)

Description of bridal gown

Description of attendants' costumes

Name of minister

Name of soloist (if any)

Where couple will honeymoon

Where couple will reside after wedding

If either the bride's or the groom's parents are divorced, the wording would be, "The bride is the daughter of [the groom is the son of] Mrs. Alicia Adams of West Palm Beach, Florida and Mr. James Adams of Los Angeles, California . . ." If one of the parents is deceased he or she is mentioned in this way: "The bride is the daughter of [the groom is the son of] Mrs. Alicia Adams [Mr. James Adams] and the late Mr. Adams [Mrs. Adams]."

Announcements of a second marriage may be sent to the newspaper, just as for a first marriage. They are similar to those of a first marriage, with the name of the former spouse and previous marital status of both bride and groom included, if desired, but no longer required.

Use this space to plan the wording of the announcement if your newspaper does not send you a form to fill out.